To Emily Lea Bock
Easter 1993
from Mommy & Daddy

THE EASTER STORY

Retold & illustrated by

CAROL HEYER

Ideals Children's Books • *Nashville, Tennessee*

Published by Ideals Publishing Corporation

Nelson Place at Elm Hill Pike

Nashville, Tennessee 37214

Printed and bound in the United States of America

Library of Congress Cataloging–in–Publication Data

Heyer, Carol, 1950–

    The Easter story / retold and illustrated by Carol Heyer.

      p.   cm.

    Summary: A biography of Jesus Christ, focusing on the events of Palm Sunday, the Last Supper, the crucifixion, and the resurrection.

    ISBN 0–8249–8439–0

    1. Jesus Christ--Resurrection--Juvenile literature.   2. Jesus Christ--Passion--Juvenile literature.   [1. Jesus Christ--Passion.

2. Bible Stories--N.T.   3. Easter.]   I. Title.

BT481.H49 1990

232.9'7--dc20   89–49056

                                   CIP

                                   AC

The illustrations in this book are rendered in acrylic paints and using live models.

The text type was set in Garamond #3.

The display type was set in Bauer Text Initials.

Color separations were made by Rayson Films, Inc. of Waukesha, Wisconsin.

Printed and bound by Worzalla Publishing Company, Stevens Point, Wisconsin.

TO MY PARENTS, MERLYN AND BILL HEYER, AS A SMALL ACKNOWLEDGMENT OF THEIR BOUNDLESS LOVE AND SUPPORT; AND FOR MY SISTER, SUZAN. AND SPECIAL THANKS TO DAVID ATKINSON, SUZAN DAVIS ATKINSON, AND DARCI ANN EVANS.

– C.H.

At Eastertime we think of fresh new grass and baby animals and warm, golden sunshine. We think of baskets full of candy and brilliantly colored eggs. But most of all, at Eastertime we think about Jesus and all that he did for us.

*J*esus was born in a manger in Bethlehem on the first Christmas Day. A great star shone in the sky above the stable, and its sparkling light led shepherds and great kings alike to Baby Jesus. They brought gifts and knelt to worship the newborn child, the Son of God.

Many, many years before, the prophets had foretold that this birth would take place and that God's Son would save the world.

When Jesus grew to be a man, he traveled across the country healing the sick and the lame and teaching about God. Everywhere Jesus went, people gathered to hear him speak. And little children flocked around him because he greeted them with love and kindness.

When the time came for Jesus to fulfill the teachings of the early prophets, he journeyed to the city of Jerusalem with his closest followers, the disciples. Jesus rode into the city on a little donkey, and people lined the streets to see him. They laid palm branches on the ground to make a soft carpet for his donkey's feet.

Jesus entered the city of Jerusalem surrounded by love and glory on this, the first Palm Sunday.

Upon his entry into Jerusalem, Jesus went straight to the temple, where he expected to find people worshiping. Instead, he found merchants buying and selling and trying to make money. Jesus was so angry that he threw the money boxes into the air and chased the merchants away. Then Jesus entered the temple to teach and to pray.

The leaders of the temple saw this and saw the crowd draw closer to hear Jesus' teachings, and they began to turn against him.

Inside the temple, Jesus told wonderful stories called parables and debated the law with the chief priests and the elders of the temple. The leaders of the temple did not like to see the people listening so closely to Jesus, so they asked him questions and tried to trick him into saying something wrong.

When asked what was the greatest commandment of all, Jesus answered, "Love God with all your heart. And this I give you as a new commandment: Love your neighbor as yourself."

As Jesus continued his teachings and more and more people followed him, the leaders and chief priests grew more fearful of him. They began to plot against Jesus and looked for a way to have him arrested.

On the night of the Feast of Unleavened Bread, Jesus and his twelve disciples gathered together for the traditional Passover meal. When they were all seated around the table, Jesus took a loaf of bread and gave thanks to God. He tore the bread into pieces and gave them to his disciples. He then passed around the cup so that each disciple could drink.

Jesus knew that this would be the last time he would sit and eat with the disciples, but he asked them to remember him in the future by gathering together to share this meal. This was Jesus' last supper.

After supper, Jesus and some of his disciples went to the Garden of Gethsemane, and Jesus went off by himself to pray. When he returned, he found that his followers had fallen asleep. As he tried to awaken them, a large crowd of people arrived, carrying torches and weapons. Sent by the chief priests, these men arrested Jesus and took him away.

The men took him to the court of Caiaphas, the high priest, where all the chief priests and elders had assembled. Caiaphas asked Jesus, "Are you Christ, the Son of God?"

When Jesus replied, "Yes, it is as you say," those assembled ordered him to be taken to the high Roman court and brought before Pilate.

As it was customary to release one prisoner each Passover, Pilate went to the people and asked if they wanted him to release Jesus. But the chief priests had stirred up the crowd, and the people angrily shouted for Jesus' death.

Pilate let the crowd take Jesus away and the soldiers put him on a cross. While the soldiers waited for him to die, Jesus' friends gathered around the cross trying to comfort each other. As Jesus' death grew near, the day seemed to turn into night. Thunder roared and lightning pierced the darkness of the sky.

And then, at the moment of Jesus' death, a powerful earthquake shook the ground so hard that the great curtain of the temple was torn in half.

Later in the day, one of Jesus' followers took down his body and tenderly laid it in a tomb. A huge, heavy stone was rolled in front of the opening, and a soldier was sent to stand guard.

Early Sunday morning, the third day after Jesus' death, a group of women brought spices to the tomb to anoint Jesus' body. But they found that the stone had been rolled away; and when they entered the tomb, they saw that Jesus' body was gone. The women were angry and afraid, and they cried out, wondering who would have taken Jesus away.

Suddenly, a man dressed all in white appeared. He asked the women, "Why do you look for the living among the dead? He is not here. He is risen!"

The women ran to tell the
disciples of the disappearance of Jesus'
body. When they heard the news, two of
the disciples returned to the tomb with
one of the women, Mary Magdalene.
They entered the tomb and found strips
of linen lying on the ground and the
burial clothes folded neatly nearby. The
disciples left the tomb feeling sad and
afraid because Jesus had been taken away.

Mary Magdalene remained alone outside the tomb weeping. As she sobbed, she heard a man's voice ask her "Why do you cry?"

Not looking up, she replied, "Sir, if you have taken Jesus away, please tell me where you have put him."

Then the man said, "Mary," and she lifted her head to see Jesus standing before her. Jesus was alive and talking to her.

Mary ran to tell the disciples, who rejoiced to know that Jesus was risen.

When Jesus met once more with his friends, he said to them, "Go throughout the whole world. Tell all the people what you have seen and heard. And remember, wherever you go, I will be there with you always, even until the end of time."

*T*his is why Christians celebrate Easter. We remember that Jesus gave up his life because he loved us. And on Easter morning, we rejoice because Jesus Christ rose from the dead and lives. And we know that because of him, we too can live.